Critical CIO Management Skills

Decision Making Skills That Every CIO Needs To Have In Order To Be Able To Make The Right Choices

"Practical, proven techniques that will show you how to manage your IT department in order to make it successful"

Dr. Jim Anderson

Published by:
Blue Elephant Consulting
Tampa, Florida

Copyright © 2013 by Dr. Jim Anderson

All rights reserved. No part of this book may be reproduced of transmitted in any form or by any means, electronic or mechanical, including photocopying, recording or by any information storage and retrieval system without written permission of the publisher, except for inclusion of brief quotations in a review.

Printed in the United States of America

Library of Congress Control Number: 2013957207

ISBN-13: 978-1494422288
ISBN-10: 149442228X

Warning – Disclaimer

The purpose of this book is to educate and entertain. This book does not promise or guarantee that anyone following the ideas, tips, suggestions, techniques or strategies will be successful. The author, publisher and distributor(s) shall have neither liability nor responsibility to anyone with respect to any loss or damage caused, or alleged to be caused, directly or indirectly by the information contained in this book.

Recent Books By The Author

Product Management

- Product Development Lessons For Product Managers: How Product Managers Can Create Successful Products

- Customer Lessons For Product Managers: Techniques For Product Managers To Better Understand What Their Customers Really Want

Public Speaking

- How To Give A Great Presentation: Presentation techniques that will transform a speech into a memorable event

- How To Rehearse In Order To Give The Perfect Speech: How to effectively rehearse your next speech to that your message be remembered forever!

CIO Skills

- How CIOs Can Make Innovation Happen: Tips And Techniques For CIOs To Use In Order To Make Innovation Happen In Their IT Department

- CIO Communication Skills Secrets: Tips And Techniques For CIOs To Use In Order To Become Better Communicators

IT Manager Skills

- Secrets Of Effective Leadership For IT Managers: Tips And Techniques That IT Managers Can Use In Order To Develop Leadership Skills

- IT Manager Career Secrets: Tips And Techniques That IT Managers Can Use In Order To Have A Successful Career

Negotiating

- Learn How To Argue In Your Next Negotiation: How To Develop The Skill Of Effective Arguing In A Negotiation In Order To Get The Best Possible Outcome

- How To Open Your Next Negotiation: How To Start A Negotiation In Order To Get The Best Possible Outcome

Miscellaneous

- Power Distribution Unit (PDU) Secrets: What Everyone Who Works In A Data Center Needs To Know!

- Making The Jump: How To Land Your Dream Job When You Get Out Of College!

Note: See a complete list of books by Dr. Jim Anderson at the back of this book.

Acknowledgements

Any book like this one is the result of years of real-world work experience. In my over 25 years of working for 7 different firms, I have met countless fantastic people and I've been mentored by some truly exceptional ones. Although I've probably forgotten some of the people who made me the person that I am today, here is my attempt to finally give them the recognition that they so truly deserve:

- Thomas P. Anderson
- Art Puett
- Bobbi Marshall
- Bob Boggs

Dr. Jim Anderson

This book is dedicated to my wife Lori. None of this would have been possible without her love and support.

Thanks for the best 21 years of my life (so far)...!

Speaking.   Negotiating.   Managing.   Marketing.

Table Of Contents

JUST EXACTLY HOW DO CIOS MANAGE? 8

ABOUT THE AUTHOR 10

CHAPTER 1: IT JUDGMENT CALLS: HOW TO MAKE GOOD ONES 15

CHAPTER 2: DID MICROSOFT PROFIT FROM HAVING STEVE BALLMER TAKE TOTAL CONTROL? 18

CHAPTER 3: BREAKTHROUGH IT STRATEGY: TAKE A NEW "PATH" TO SUCCESS 21

CHAPTER 4: I.T.I.S. (IT'S THE INFORMATION, STUPID!) 25

CHAPTER 5: IN IT, BIGGER IS NOT NECESSARILY BETTER 28

CHAPTER 6: WHAT CAN IT LEARN FROM HOW CHRYSLER MAKES CARS? 31

CHAPTER 7: NETFLIX SHIPPING PROBLEMS: THE IT HORROR STORY! 35

CHAPTER 8: W.W.N.M.D.?: WHAT WOULD NELSON MANDELA DO? 40

CHAPTER 9: OUT OF TIME, OUT OF TALENT – WHY IT DEPARTMENTS FAIL 44

CHAPTER 10: WICKED, WICKED IT STRATEGY PROBLEMS 47

CHAPTER 11: MANAGING WICKED IT PROBLEMS 51

CHAPTER 12: WICKED WAYS OF MANAGING WICKED IT PROBLEMS 54

Just Exactly How Do CIOs Manage?

What does it really mean to be a CIO? You sure won't be writing any software any more. You won't be stringing network cables or updating firewall parameters. What does a CIO really do? I've got some bad news for you: CIOs manage.

Sure, we all think that we know what that word means, but when it comes down to what CIOs do on a daily basis, what does this mean? At its very simplest, to manage means to make decisions. Not just any decisions, but the right decisions over and over again. That's why the really good CIOs get paid the big bucks.

How can we learn to make the right management decisions? Judgment calls are a skill that can be learned, you just have to know how to go about doing it. We can look to companies such as Microsoft to get an understanding of how they go about doing it. However, we need to keep in mind that in the world of IT, bigger does not always mean better.

Your company's IT department is built around one thing: information. It's how you collect it, store it, and use it that will determine how successful a CIO you are. This means that you need to be learning from how other companies have accomplished this and you need to be avoiding the mistakes that they have made.

Finally, in the world of IT not all problems are created equally. There is a special breed of problems that we call "wicked" problems that are so big and so tough that all of our normal management skills generally don't work on them. They require a new way of thinking in order to solve.

This book is going to provide you with the management skills that you are going to need as a CIO in order to be successful. We'll be taking a look at other firms and how they've dealt with management challenges (both successfully and unsuccessfully) and several new approaches that you can use will be revealed.

For more information on what it takes to be a great CIO, check out my blog, The Accidental Successful CIO, at:

www.TheAccidentalSuccessfulCIO.com

Good luck!

- Dr. Jim Anderson

About The Author

I must confess that I never set out to be a CIO. When I went to school, I studied Computer Science and thought that I'd get a nice job programming and that would be that. Well, at least part of that plan worked out!

My first job was working for Boeing on their F/A-18 fighter jet program. I spent my days programming fighter jet software in assembly language and I loved it. The U.S. government decided to save some money and went looking for other countries to sell this plane to. This put me into an unfamiliar role: I started to meet with foreign military officials and I ended up having to manage groups of engineers who were working on international projects.

Time moved on and so did I. I found myself working for Siemens, the big German telecommunications company. They were making phone switches and selling them to the seven U.S. phone companies. The problem was that the switches were too complicated. Customers couldn't tell the difference between one complicated phone switch from another complicated phone switch. Once again I found myself working with the sales and marketing teams to find ways to make the great technology that the engineers had developed understandable to both internal and external customers.

I've spent over 25 years working as an senior IT professional for both big companies and startups. This has given me an opportunity to learn what it takes to manage and IT department in ways that allow it to maximize its output while becoming a valuable part of the overall company.

I now live in Tampa Florida where I spend my time managing my consulting business, Blue Elephant Consulting, teaching college courses at the University of South Florida, and traveling to work with companies like yours to share the knowledge that I have about how to create and manage successful IT departments.

I'm always available to answer questions and I can be reached at:

Dr. Jim Anderson
Blue Elephant Consulting
Email: jim@BlueElephantConsulting.com
Facebook: http://goo.gl/1TVoK
Web: www.BlueElephantConsulting.com

"Unforgettable communication skills that will set your ideas free..."

Create IT Departments That Are Productive And A Valuable Asset To The Rest Of The Company !

Dr. Jim Anderson is available to provide training and coaching on the topics that are the most important to people who have to manage IT departments: how can I build a productive IT department (and keep it together) while at the same time providing the rest of the company with the IT services that they need?

Dr. Anderson believes that in order to both learn and remember what he says, speakers need to laugh. Each one of his speeches is full of fun and humor so that what he says "sticks" with everyone.

Dr. Anderson's CIO SkillsTraining Includes:

1. How to identify and attract the right type of IT workers to your IT department.
2. How to build relationships with the company's senior management in order to get the support that you need?
3. How to stay on top of changing technology and security issues so that you never get surprised?

Dr. Jim Anderson works with over 100 customers per year. To invite Dr. Anderson to work with you, contact him at:

Phone: 813-418-6970 or
Email: jim@BlueElephantConsulting.com

Blue Elephant Consulting
Speaking. Negotiating. Managing. Marketing.

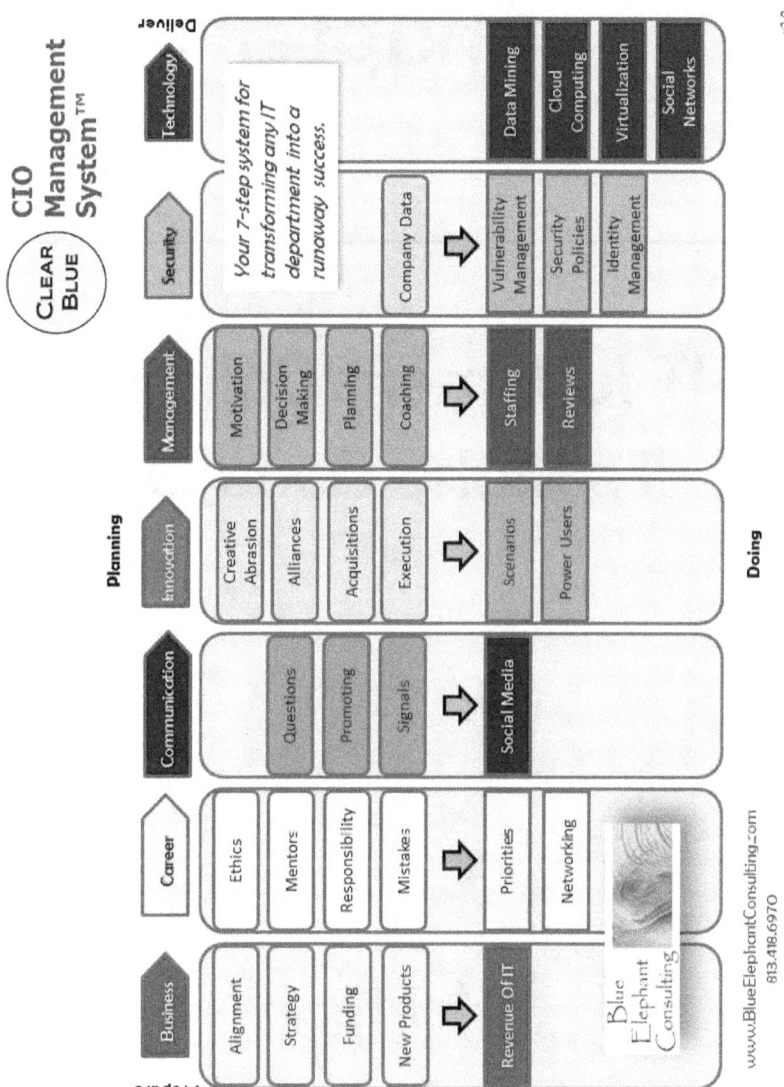

The **Clear Blue CIO Management System™** has been created to provide CIOs and senior IT managers with a clear roadmap for how to manage an IT department. This system shows CIOs what needs to be done and in what order to do it.

Chapter 1

IT Judgment Calls: How To Make Good Ones

Chapter 1: IT Judgment Calls: How To Make Good Ones

Warren Bennis is a smart guy (professor of business administration and chairman of the leadership Institute at the University of Southern California). He's cranked out a book called **Judgment: How Winning Leaders Make Great Calls** and it has a few ideas that really relate to today's IT leadership environment.

It turns out that the ability to make good judgment calls when you are a CIO is very important (surprise!) because of the impact on others that all of your decisions make. When do these CIOs get called on to make judgment calls?

Warrne identified of the most common three areas: people, strategy, and what to do in a crises. We see the impacts of people judgments around us at work every day. Technically gifted folks who get put into a management role for which they are poorly suited, great team leaders who get bumped up and become Directors, etc.

The successes in choosing the right people for the right job get reflected on the company's bottom line. The mistakes can cause lots of damage and are expensive to replace and to repair.

Strategy judgments are the big ones that can make or break a career. In today's hyperactive IT environment speed is often prized over accuracy. Warren brings up a great IT example in his book: Intel.

Many folks don't realize this, but Intel got its start in manufacturing and selling memory chips. When the prices in this market started eroding and the Japanese manufacturers started coming on strong, Intel had to make a judgment call: stay in the memory chip business or move on to something else? Gordon Moore and Andy Grove made the decision to move on (to CPUs) and the rest, as they say, is history. Good judgment call.

Finally, the ability to make good judgment calls in in middle of a crisis. Once again Intel serves as a good IT example.

Back in 1994, as Intel was releasing the latest version of their x86 chip line it was discovered that under certain circumstances it would return the incorrect answer from a math operation. Initially Intel took the IT road in its response: it did some math and stated that the average user would only see an error once every 27,000 years.

However, that didn't sit well with most of their customers and eventually Intel had to offer to refund/replace the defective chips. This initial response was a very, very poor judgment call on Intel's part.

So what can IT leaders do to make better judgment calls? Warren suggests that we work on improving four areas of our knowledge that are critical to making good judgment calls: self-knowledge, social-network knowledge, organizational knowledge, and stakeholder knowledge. Hmm, sure sounds like aligning the IT organization with the rest of the business would go a long way to making this a reality!

Chapter 2

Did Microsoft Profit From Having Steve Ballmer Take Total Control?

Chapter 2: Did Microsoft Profit From Having Steve Ballmer Take Total Control?

The news is a bit old by now; however, it's still a big deal that Steve Ballmer has decided to retire as Microsoft's CEO. I believe that Microsoft employs over 100,000 staff and so Steve had his hands full while he was in charge trying to find a way (or ways) to once again make Microsoft more agile. Time will have to be the judge as to if he was successful in picking a path for the company to follow while he was in charge: strategy, quality, or innovation.

What would you have done if you had been in Steve's IT shoes? Microsoft has a fundamental dilemma: are they one huge company (a la Wal-Mart) or are they a loosely connected set of business units (a la GE)? The key point to remember here is that Microsoft is neither a Wal-Mart nor a GE so whatever path they take, they will need to create their own unique structure.

In terms of major projects, the next release of the Windows operating system cannot happen quickly enough. No matter what you think of Windows 8, the public perception of it is that it is undesirable. The next CEO can put his or her best people on it and see if they can turn this perception around or they can simply quickly release the next version and consider Windows 8 a horrible learning experience.

Next Microsoft still seems to be interested in getting into the mobile phone market. I'm not sure if this is simply a case of *"We can do whatever Apple can do…"* or if they really see it as a key pillar of their growth. No matter what, they need to put some creative talent onto this one. They've got a powerful lever in the Exchange email tool — if they can build on that, they could have a leg to stand on.

Finally, the next CEO has got to realize that the Internet is all about search. Right now it looks like the company still maneuvering to get a piece of Yahoo's search business using their Bing tool. Perhaps what the next CEO really should be doing is looking further out and finding out where Google is NOT the dominate search engine and spend some of those Microsoft R&D dollars to attack Google from the outside instead of going head-to-head with them.

Chapter 3

Breakthrough IT Strategy: Take A New "Path" To Success

Chapter 3: Breakthrough IT Strategy: Take A New "Path" To Success

Businesses today spent roughly 5% of their gross revenue on IT and end up with very little to show for it. A couple of very bright guys over at the Harvard Business School (David Upton and Bradley Staats) have come up with a new approach to Enterprise IT Projects. They started their research from Eric Raymond's (programmer / open source champion) point-of-view: most IT projects are built using the Cathedral Approach:

- they cost a lot,
- they take a really long time to create,
- and they only start to deliver any value after they are all done.

The Harvard guys believe that they have come up with a different approach that slashes costs while at the same time boosting the existing business and even making it easier to launch new ones. Sound interesting?

The new IT strategy is called the "path" approach. It assumes that there is no way that you can define all of a system's specifications at the start of a project and so instead you just focus on laying out a path for the system to be further developed over time.

As a proof that this approach works, they studied the Shinsei Bank which is a Japanese bank. In 1998 Shinsei was in a bad spot: it had had gone bust and (due to bad loans — sound familiar?) had been sold to the U.S. private equity firm Ripplewood Holdings.

The very smart guys at Ripplewood got Masamoto Yashiro (former chairman of Citigroup Japan) to be the CEO of this struggling bank. Yashiro decided that Sinsei needed to compete based on a strong IT department. Here's how they used a path-based approach to do it:

- Instead of implementing a new "big bang" set of business software, they took a different approach. They build a modular infrastructure that would allow them to put pieces in as needed.

- They built new systems that mimicked the old existing systems that the bank was already using. This allowed them to switch folks over to the new system and then make gradual improvements without requiring extensive retraining.

- They helped to ensure that the IT department was integrated with Sinsei's business strategy by having the CIO report directly to the CEO. Note that this is different from many U.S. firms where the CIO reports to the CFO and is effectively "hidden" from the CEO.

- The Sinsei business unit heads spend a lot of time learning to "talk IT". This helps to break down internal communication barriers.

- Sinsei IT application development projects start by focusing on the foreseeable business objectives — not the existing business environment. In other words, they think about how they want things to work, not about how they can automate how things currently work. The IT strategy is then built to meet this forecasted future.

- This is key: the Sinsei business folks tell IT what they need. IT creates prototypes and has the business side use them. This causes feedback and new possible solutions are identified.

Finally, the Harvard boys identified three characteristics of a path based IT solution that will allow it to succeed:

- **Use a minimal set of standards**: pick a few and stay with them. This will reduce costs and simplify the entire project.

- **Create Simple Reusable Solutions:** This can be as simple as taking each IT problem, breaking it down as far as it can possibly go, and then implementing solutions to those individual problems. When the low-level problems are connected together you'll have a flexible solution that can be easily adjusted if any component changes.

- **Create Solutions With Modularity, Not Just Modules**: Getting back to the original definition of modules, this simply means that you can tinker inside of one module without impacting any of the other modules that make up a complete solution. A good example of this is to create a solution that can be rolled out in phases. This limits your risk, allows users to get used to the new business software, and allows time for changes to be made.

The Harvard boys concluded their study with one final note of caution: if you want to build on what you've accomplished with an IT project, then you need to ensure that you have the committed involvement of your end-users. Otherwise you can expect to fail.

In the end, the Shinsei bank is doing quite well due in part to its strong IT department. We need to realize that most large IT projects end up failing due to internal resistance instead of any technology issues. The use of the path based approach to IT projects has allowed Shinsei bank to completely re-invent itself while avoiding traditional big IT project problems.

Chapter 4

I.T.I.S. (It's The Information, Stupid!)

Chapter 4: I.T.I.S. (It's The Information, Stupid!)

Q: What's wrong with IT departments today?

A: They don't look or act like any other department in the rest of the company.

One glaring example of this rears its ugly head when business users ask for company information and the IT team responds with a discussion about the technology that either interconnects it or simply collects it. It turns out that there is a big difference between information (a.k.a. knowledge) and data.

IT departments do a great job of collecting a lot of data; however, that's not what anyone wants. What everyone wants is information – what you get when you process the data.

Somehow we need to come up with a way to get IT departments to shift their focus from gathering more data to providing more information services that will help the business do better.

Three professors, Arik Ragowsky, Paul Licker, and David Gefen have spent some time studying this issue and asking question such as what is the real job of a CIO? It turns out that a CIO should be spending his/her time managing the information that the company depends on in order to be successful in its business.

What this means is that CIOs have to find a way to change their thinking and move away from worrying about how to deliver more data and start to think about how to provide more information services.

How did IT end up being a plumber and not an architect? Back in the old days (1960's), all computers were mainframes and business folks had no idea how IT folks did what they did.

However, they appreciated what the Information Systems (IS) department produced and were more than willing to pay for them to keep doing it. When PCs arrived in the early 80's, suddenly everyone knew more about how computers worked.

IS was renamed to Information Technology (IT) and the IT folks started to focus more on the technology and less on the information that the technology was delivering. Vendors helped things along by starting to sell directly to end users. This is when things got all messed up!

Who's to blame for the current situation? Well, we IT departments have more than our fair share to bear.

All too often we interact with business customers using technology terms. When we do this we are seen as the "geeks" that we really are instead of business partners.

What we should be doing is talking business with the business folks and reserving our technology discussions for when we are back within the IT department and talking with our teammates.

Final thought: hide the technology and the data from the business customers. Instead, talk with them about information systems and the types of information that they need in order to help the company be successful.

Chapter 5

In IT, Bigger is NOT Necessarily Better

Chapter 5: In IT, Bigger is NOT Necessarily Better

Way back in my young & foolish days I had the opportunity to work at a couple of startups. I came to them after having worked for very large firms such as Boeing, Siemens, and Alcatel. Needless to say the environment, attitude, and overall energy level at the startups was completely different from the large established firms.

One of my friends from those days, Charlie, has moved on and the startup that he's working for can no longer really be called a startup: they've got 800 employees and have been around for almost 10 years now. Thanks to LinkedIn we've reconnected and we got to talking about the "good 'ol days".

What caught my attention is that Charlie told me that he's been put in charge of a project to rekindle the "startup spirit" within his company. When I asked him how he was going to go about doing that, he said that he had no good ideas.

Charlie's firm is struggling with the same issue that Microsoft is dealing with: how can a large firm with lots of resources learn to operate like a smaller, more nimble firm? Everyone realizes that Google, Facebook, Salesforce.com, etc. weren't born inside of a large firm.

Instead, they started life as a startup and because they had a great product and lots of employee energy, they got lucky and have become successful. Just about every large company would like to find a way to infuse itself with that kind of "startup energy" (a.k.a. innovation).

Janet Rae-Dupree wrote a piece dealing with this topic for the New York Times awhile back. Some interesting observations came out of this article.

The first is that just about everyone agrees that when it comes to IT and innovation, bigger is not always better. Specifically, smaller teams that are made up of staff from different departments seem to be able to move much quicker than larger traditional organizations.

Specifically decisions get made much faster and so the entire team is able to move on to the next-next-next thing. I can hear collective HR and Legal departments gasping at the thought right now!

I almost hate to say it, but the TV show Survivor has proved this point. When forced to, people can work together to solve complex problems in unique ways.

Yeah, yeah – there will always be backstabbing and alliances formed; however, when the team's survival depends on its success this can overcome many of these personality issues.

As Charlie and I wrapped up our talk, I pointed out the Survivor analogy to him. He pushed back and said that he liked the small team idea but didn't want to be kicking employees off of an island each week.

I told that he didn't need to do that, but what he could do is limit the resources available to a team (time, money, etc.) and tell them that they need to reach a milestone before one of their resources ran out. If they didn't then the team would be disbanded. Everyone works better under startup-like pressures!

Chapter 6

What Can IT Learn From How Chrysler Makes Cars?

Chapter 6: What Can IT Learn From How Chrysler Makes Cars?

Although working in IT can be a tough job at times, I must confess that working in the American car manufacturing industry sure seems like it is probably a much rougher place to work at times. I'm always interested in what's going on in the car biz because once upon a time I almost ended up going to the General Motors Institute (now known as Kettering University) and probably would have ended up going to work in the car industry.

We've talked before about what IT management can learn from the people who brought us the subprime mess. Now it's the good folks at Chrysler are starting to do some interesting things that have caught my attention and I think that they may now be in a position to teach us something.

First, just a bit of background information for anyone who hasn't been keep up with current events. The private equity firm Cerberus Capital Management bought Chrysler for about $7.4B. What this means is that Chrysler is no longer a publicly traded company – Cerberus can do pretty much whatever they want and don't have to answer to anyone.

Except the people who put up the $7.4B. Who want to see a return on their investment as quickly as possible.

So why did Cerberus buy Chrysler. In short, they think that they can do a better job of running Chrysler than the previous management did.

If they are correct, then they can make the company profitable and take it public and make much more than $7.4B. The trick is to do this as quickly as possible. If they can't pull this off, then they could end up shutting Chrysler down and just walking away from their $7.4B investment. Got that?

Ok, so now we move up to current time. Robert Nardelli is the CEO of Chrysler and he was brought in from after being the CEO of The Home Depot. What this means is that he's not a "car guy" and he's not limited in his thinking by how things have been done in the past.

Shortly after Cerberus bought Chrysler new stories started to circulate about Chrysler having talks with Nissan about partnering to jointly produce midsize cars. This is a possible fundamental shift in how Chrysler makes and sells cars.

Basically, Nissan would design, engineer, and manufacture the cars and then Chrysler would sell them under their own name. This could save Chrysler the billions of dollars that it takes to create a new car. Not content to put all of its eggs in one basket, Chrysler has also entered into a partnership with China's Cherry Automobile Co. who will be making small cars for them.

News reporters were quick to point out that this model has worked well for others such as Dell and Nike who really don't do engineering and manufacturing, but rather focus on marketing and selling. This approach has been tried in the auto industry before; however, these efforts have not panned out well for a number of ill-defined reasons.

So what does this all mean for IT executives? Perhaps it's time to slay some of our sacred cows and stop doing software development and stop doing routine support activities.

Instead, perhaps these activities should be completely outsourced and our IT shops should retool to focus on what we should be doing best: supporting the business.

Specifically, if like Cerberus we would be motivated by the need to have the business turn a profit quickly, we could focus on working with the business units and try to understand what their issues are and how IT tools and technology can be used to solve these problems.

What would happen if Cerberus took over your IT shop? Just imagine if the job of an IT shop was to create very detailed product requirements and to perform testing on products that were created based on those requirements.

Can you imagine just how close the IT shop could get to the business? The invisible wall between IT and the business side of the house would come crashing down. When old ways of doing business ("everything is invented here") are torn down and replaced with new ways ("we focus on only what we do best and outsource everything else") then that can truly transform the way IT does business.

Chapter 7

Netflix Shipping Problems: The IT Horror Story!

Chapter 7: Netflix Shipping Problems: The IT Horror Story!

Just in case you haven't heard the news, a while back Netflix basically shut down due to some mysterious internal problem that halted their ability to ship DVDs. This is fascinating news – it's similar to having FedEx announce that they had halted delivery of packages because they couldn't figure out where they were supposed to go. What's going on here?

Netflix has 8.5 million subscribers who pay a monthly fee to rent DVD movies. The movies that they select are delivered by mail and when they are returned by mail, then the next movie in the subscriber's queue is mailed to them.

From an IT point of view, the heart of the company is their database(s). This truly is an information based company.

I have been a happy subscriber for at least 5 years now and I've never had a problem with getting my movies. For Netflix to come out and admit that they are having a problem (I've even received an email from them) must mean that the problem has existed for several days and they now felt the need to tell the world before people started wondering where their next movie is.

Clearly this kind of outage is going to cost the company – Citi analyst Tony Wible is guessing that the tab will be $1.8 million to $3.6 million in revenue a day. Talk about a melt-down!

One possible source of Netflix's problems might be the simple fact that they don't appear to have a CIO! A quick search of both the company web site and Hoovers turned up no likely suspects. Hmm, perhaps this IT ship has nobody at the helm!

Back to the problem — I have no secret insight into how Netflix runs their business. However, Tom Dillon, who had been serving as the company's COO as well as its CIO, gave some interviews and from these we can piece parts of the story together.

At the core of Netflix's operations is the ability to automate as much of the process of sending and receiving DVDs as possible. Since the solution that they have in place to automate these tasks is proprietary, it is of course a trade secret.

However, we do have some information. When a DVD comes in, the first thing that is done is to check it to make sure the right disk is in the right sleeve. Next, the serial number on the jacket is scanned.

Now that Netflix's proprietary software knows what DVD it's dealing with, it can consider the company's total inventory of that title, the next items on customers' wish lists of movies they want to see, and a host of other factors. At this time, the DVD will either be sent out again, be placed in inventory or simply retired.

When things are working correctly, Netflix says that it is able to check in a returned DVD and send out a new one within one day more than 90% of the time. The two challenges that Netflix has always been open about are scaling issues and bottlenecks.

As Netflix has rapidly grown in the number of subscribers that it has to serve and the number of movies that it has in its inventory, IT challenges will occur. Additionally, bottlenecks in the DVD processing and delivery process can occur at any time.

Dillon admitted that bottlenecks can't be predicted and basically just have to be dealt with as they show up. If Netflix stumbles, the problem will quickly go from bad to worse. The reason is that they receive over 100,000 new disks a day.

So what could have gone so terribly, terribly wrong here? I'm just taking a guess, but based on years of experience in IT I'm thinking that we're looking at a cascading problem that was started by a software upgrade.

A good guess as to how this all started is that some relatively minor piece of Netflix's proprietary automation system got a routine update. Next, some sequence of events occurred that caused this updated software to fail or behave in some unexpected way.

This problem then cascaded up and down the automated DVD processing line. Since Netflix is reporting that all of their distribution centers are impacted, this means that either a core system is down, or they performed the upgrade at each site at the same time.

As horrible as this must be for Netflix, it's not the first time we've seen this type of problem: AT&T has had its frame-relay network shut down due to software issues, XM Radio took a hit for two days, JetBlue's unromantic Valentine's Day outage, and of course, any Blackberry outage ends up being front page news.

Netflix is reporting that they have their entire technical staff trying to fix this problem. This means that the original issue spread to multiple applications and may have damaged their corporate data.

Now that we're done pointing fingers, what could have Netflix done to prevent this from happening in the first place?

1. **Have An "Undo" Button**: Most IT shops keep an old version of each application in storage even after it has been replaced. If the updated software starts to cause problems, then the old version can be rolled back out and reinstalled.

- **Don't Put All Eggs In Single Basket**: If indeed Netflix updated all of their distribution operations at the same time, then they were foolish indeed. Instead, upgrades should be done to a single site first in order to determine if there are any unknown issues. Dealing with a single site that is down is much easier than having all of your sites down.

- **In Case Of Emergency, Go Manual**: Although I love automation as much as the next IT worker, it's always a good idea to know how to perform the automated tasks by hand just in case there is a day that this might be required. Since Netflix has reported that they are down, not just limping along, clearly they don't have a manual process to fall back on.

I'm confident that Netflix will solve this problem (but nobody there gets to sleep until they do!); however, after the problem is fixed they are going to have to make some changes in their IT shop in order to ensure that this never happens again. Good luck!

Chapter 8

W.W.N.M.D.?: What Would Nelson Mandela Do?

Chapter 8: W.W.N.M.D.?: What Would Nelson Mandela Do?

So what's a CIO to do when they get plopped down in the middle of a battlefield? No matter if internal strife has caused different sides of the house to stop playing together or if a merger has physically brought together teams but not made them members of the same department, a CIO has his/her work cut out for them as they try to make the correct judgment calls and forge a single unified department before their time runs out and they are shown the door.

Nelson Mandela found himself in a similar situation in 1994 after South Africa held its first free elections. Mandela's party had won the election and he was now the president of South Africa.

However, he had been elected by the black voters and this meant that the white voters felt alienated. This created a dangerous situation for South Africa because the whites retained both money and weapons and they could rise up and take down Mandela's fledgling new government if they felt threatened.

In his book, "**Playing The Enemy**", John Carlin talks about what Mandela did to diffuse this volatile situation and I believe that it contains a number of lessons for CIOs who find themselves in the middle of a business civil war.

In Mandela's case, the game of rugby was a game of the white minority that blacks had pushed for the world to boycott while the previous government was in power. Now that Mandela was president, he reached out to the country's rugby establishment and offered to host the 1995 World Cup rugby games in South Africa.

Mandela then worked to associate himself and his personal charisma to the game of rugby and by doing this he hoped to get all of South Africa excited about trying to win the world championship.

It was in this way that Nelson Mandela was able to get both sides to take the first few tentative steps together away from chaos and towards unity.

It was Mandela who said *"You don't address their brains, you address their hearts."* CIOs can learn a great deal from all of this. When placed in a situation where there are multiple warring sides, a good CIO needs to move quickly to diffuse the situation.

Any time, energy, or effort that is being spent on fighting an internal war will take away from the goal of the IT department which is to help the company move forward. The longer that the department spends battling within itself, then the greater the risk that the rest of the company will determine that it is more of a burden to the company than an asset.

So a great discussion so far, but what's a CIO to do? Here are three suggestions for tackling a civil war situation head on and coming out a winner:

- **Do It The Mandela Way**: Identify which side is the weaker side (perhaps the purchased company's IT department). Then do some research and find out what unique event, process, or reward that department used to have which unified it before the civil war broke out. Finally, take that unique identifier and apply it to the entire department so that they can all share in it and come together as they do.

- **Identify A Shared External Threat**: Nothing forces teams to come together better than the perception that they are under assault from the outside. If you can identify and describe a valid external condition that could severely impact the IT department then the civil war activities will be forgotten as everyone mobilizes to fend off the threat. By working together to save the department, the civil war issues may be forgotten.

- **Cross Populate**: In order to resolve civil war situations, communication between the different sides needs to start. One way to ensure that this will happen is to switch managers: management from one side is placed in charge of workers from the other side and vice versa. Although this will cause a great deal of grumbling at first, over time everyone will settle into their new roles and the distinction between "us" and "them" will become blurred and eventually go away.

There you have it – civil wars can be avoided. Nelson Mandela led South Africa through its most dangerous time and emerged victorious on the other side. CIOs who find themselves in volatile work environments can learn from what Mr. Mandela did and, hopefully, follow his lead.

Chapter 9

Out Of Time, Out Of Talent – Why IT Departments Fail

Chapter 9: Out Of Time, Out Of Talent – Why IT Departments Fail

A business stall can hit a company / IT department at any time. There can be many reasons for what causes a stall including having a premium product or abandoning a good market segment too early as a company goes looking for greener grass.

If that was all that could happen to a company, that would surely be enough. However, there is one more key contributor that can cause an otherwise successful company to lose forward momentum and go into a tailspin: they run out of talent.

In this day of IT layoffs and downsizings, it doesn't seem possible that a firm could run out of the IT talent that they need. However, it's having a lack of IT leaders and their associated staff who have the necessary IT capabilities and interpersonal skills that are so desperately needed in order to execute the company's strategy.

We're not talking about not having enough SQL knowledgeable programmers here. Rather what we are discussing is a lack of specific required capabilities that are needed by the firm.

These capabilities can include such things as the ability to sell complex IT solutions, or perhaps some special skill in marketing IT solutions to a given market segment. This lack of talent becomes most glaring when it occurs at the executive level within the company.

How Do Talent Shortages Happen? It turns out that most internal shortfalls in skills are a result of a company's too strict adherence to a "promote from within" policy.

What's interesting about this is that this situation is most often seen in companies that are lauded for their strong sense of corporate culture. This internal promotion policy serves the company poorly when the company's business environment presents it with a novel challenge or when their competition suddenly increases.

What Role Does Experience Play? A big one it turns out. Rapidly developing events in a company's market place require the company to quickly respond by modifying how it does business. Having a narrow set of experiences in the executive suite means that the company's ability to quickly respond to such changes can be severely limited.

So What's The Solution? Quick question – does your IT department have any program in place to formally monitor the balance between both company lifers vs. those who have been brought in from the outside both in the executive team and lower on down the management ladder? It's the outsiders who are going to bring in fresh approaches and perspectives.

Even if the firm does bring in outsiders, does it incorporate them into the company? Studies show that between 35%-40% of senior executives don't make it past their first 18 months.

The correct way to solve this problem is to set up a formal IT department policy that states that HR will work to ensure that there is a mix of management. A good suggestion for a mix ratio that seems to work is to ensure that there is between 10% – 30% of management that is from the outside.

Chapter 10

Wicked, Wicked IT Strategy Problems

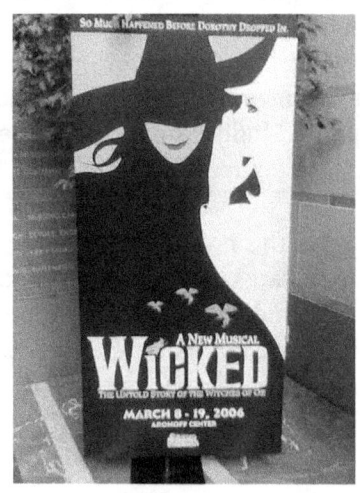

Chapter 10: Wicked, Wicked IT Strategy Problems

Some problems just can't be solved. As an IT guy with an engineering background, I find this hard to believe – it goes against my grain.

I mean, back in school I encountered lots of problems that at first blush appeared to be impossible to solve. However, once I had gotten a little deeper into whatever class I was taking at the time things started to become clearer.

New tools that I had learned could be used to solve what had previously appeared to be unsolvable problems. In the world of IT, the IT department can even help keep a company out of an economic stall and so I thought that there was no problem that an IT department couldn't solve. It turns out that real life is not nearly so neat.

Dr. John Camillus has spent the past 15 years studying how companies create their own strategies. During this time he has uncovered what he likes to call "wicked" business problems – strategy issues that are difficult because our traditional processes for solving problems just can't resolve them.

IT departments face these types of problems internally as well as facing them as part of a company's overall strategy planning process. Wicked problems can be especially trying for IT departments because they seem to resist being solved by our standard techniques of gathering more metrics, revisiting the core issues and creating a more detailed definition of them, or even the time honored technique of breaking the big problems that we can't solve down into smaller problems that we hope that we can solve.

Dr. Camillus says that not only do our traditional ways of dealing with problems not work on wicked problems, but they can also make things far worse.

Dr. Camillus recently wrote an article for the Harvard Business Review in which he discussed wicked business problems. In it he stated that organizations, like an IT department, will most likely encounter a wicked problem when they are facing either a period of constant change or have encountered challenges that are bigger then they have ever seen before.

Within an IT department, it won't just be the technological complexity that make a problem a wicked problem, but rather all of the social issues that come along with it that will turn it into a wicked problem.

How can you tell if your problem is a wicked problem? It would be nice if wicked problems came labeled as such. However, they don't.

Having the ability to identify a wicked IT problem early on can save any CIO a significant amount of time and grief. You won't be able to tell just by looking at the problem itself, but rather you have to take a look at what surrounds the problem.

Specifically, if a problem is causing confusion or discord among your IT team, and there has been a distinct lack of progress in creating a solution for it so far, then there is a good chance that you are looking at a wicked problem.

Just to make sure that you really do have a wicked problem and not one of those more common really, really hard IT problems, there are some additional criteria that you need to check before you can call a IT problem a wicked problem:

1. **Too Many People Are Involved:** A problem that has too many people who are impacted by it starts to look like a

wicked problem very quickly. Each person who has a different vested interest and is working on a different set of priorities will contribute to making a difficult problem into an unsolvable wicked one.

2. **The Cause Of The Problem Is Not Clear:** There is no single cause for the IT issue that you are dealing with. Generally there are multiple sources that have fed the problem including competition, issues with employees & staffing, company strengths that have become detriments and a traditional domestic vs. international focus can also compound the problem.

3. **The Problem Is Shaped Like A Blob:** This is an especially tricky characteristic to deal with – the problem seems to change shape every time you try to deal with it. This makes it hard to "get a grip" on the problem and so you may not have any idea as to where to start.

4. **You've Never Seen Anything Like This Before:** How can you solve a problem that doesn't look like any other problem that you've ever seen before? When you face a problem that you've never seen before, the question of what tools or techniques to use to solve it becomes even more critical.

5. **There Are No Signs Showing You The Right Direction:** Most problems come with some sort of indication of what the correct next thing to do in order to solve it is. However, wicked problems have no such indicators. You are truly on you own here.

Chapter 11

Managing Wicked IT Problems

Chapter 11: Managing Wicked IT Problems

So we've chatted about Wicked IT Strategy problems – these are the ones that you really can't solve. Given that, you've got a couple of different things that you can do.

The easiest is to throw your arms up in the air, say "this can't be solved", and then work very hard at getting promoted so that it becomes someone else's problem. Good luck with that approach! Let's take a look at some other solutions for those of us who feel a deep burning need to make the world a better place for all...

Let us acknowledge that wicked IT problems can't be solved. So your next best alternative is to come up with ways to cope with them.

They aren't going away, so you need to find some common ground that will allow you to live with them. As with all of us in IT, there are countless complicated solutions that you could probably come up with in order to address any problem. However, here are a couple of relatively simple actions that you can take that will yield real results:

Make everyone responsible for finding a way to manage the problem. This means that you need to reach out and drag in employees, customers, management, etc. and you need to make sure that you document everything that is said and establish clear a means of communication between all parties.

Because a wicked problem is so complex, it will take a wide variety of views and opinions in order to come up with unique ways of managing the problem. However, be careful! Don't just collect inputs.

Instead, make sure that everyone is involved in actually implementing their suggestions. Yes, having more people involved will make things more difficult, but because of the complexity of the problem they are all needed.

Documenting all ideas and discussions will become more important when a plan is finally agreed on – the documentation will be needed in order to communicate the plan to the rest of the department.

Define what your department's identity is. Although many different suggestions will be made as to how best to manage the wicked problem, it will be critical that whatever solutions are finally put in place are true to the IT department's identity.

The department's identity is the cornerstone of its strategy and provides both direction and focus for the IT leaders. An identity is made up of a department's values, competencies, and its aspirations. Staying true to these will allow critical decisions to be made quickly and painlessly.

Chapter 12

Wicked Ways Of Managing Wicked IT Problems

Chapter 12: Wicked Ways Of Managing Wicked IT Problems

Wicked IT problems can frustrate even the best of us – by their very nature, wicked IT problems have no solution (that's why we call them "wicked" and not just "hard"). As we talked about in the last Chapter, although you may not have the tools to solve these types of problems, you do have the tools needed to manage them.

However, the key to dealing with problems like this successfully is to involve the entire IT department (yes, these problems are really that big). Let's talk about how you'd go about doing that...

The first department-wide step that you'd need to take is to get everyone to **focus on taking action**. In traditional problem solving, we think though all of the possible strategies that we could execute and then pick the one(s) that we think will solve the problem.

Sorry – that approach doesn't work when you are dealing with a wicked problem. Instead, what you need to be doing is some experimenting. Specifically, choose a collection of strategies that you think MIGHT work and start executing them.

This approach actually has a name it's called the "science of muddling through". One thing that you're going to have to keep in mind is that every action that you take to deal with the wicked IT problem will cause the problem to change. Remember, we're dealing with a wicked problem here!

Finally, you need to take the hardest step. You need to implement what is called a **"feed forward"** process for your IT department.

We are all very familiar with feedback systems where we compare the results of our actions to our original plans and then change our actions accordingly. Once again, bad news – feedback won't help you to deal with a wicked IT problem, instead you are going to need a feed forward solution.

A feed forward process requires IT management and workers to take the time to imagine the IT department in the future. The future should be defined as being 5, 10, 25, and even 50 years down the road. The goal of this process is to picture what the IT department will be like, and then to determine what steps need to be taken today in order to move the department towards that goal.

So there you have it – ways to manage your wicked IT problems. Remember, when you encounter a frustrating IT problem, there is always the chance that it may be a wicked problem. These types of problems can't be solved and so you're going to have to practice some wicked management…

It's from the forge of failure that the steel of success is formed.

Hard Work Does Not Guarantee Success, But Success Does Not Happen Without Hard Work.

- Dr. Jim Anderson

Create IT Departments That Are Productive And A Valuable Asset To The Rest Of The Company !

Dr. Jim Anderson is available to provide training and coaching on the topics that are the most important to people who have to manage IT departments: how can I build a productive IT department (and keep it together) while at the same time providing the rest of the company with the IT services that they need?

Dr. Anderson believes that in order to both learn and remember what he says, speakers need to laugh. Each one of his speeches is full of fun and humor so that what he says "sticks" with everyone.

Dr. Anderson's CIO SkillsTraining Includes:

4. How to identify and attract the right type of IT workers to your IT department.
5. How to build relationships with the company's senior management in order to get the support that you need?
6. How to stay on top of changing technology and security issues so that you never get surprised?

Dr. Jim Anderson works with over 100 customers per year. To invite Dr. Anderson to work with you, contact him at:

Phone: 813-418-6970 or
Email: jim@BlueElephantConsulting.com

Photo Credits:

Cover - By: Nate Shivar
http://www.flickr.com/photos/nshivar/

Chapter 1 - By: Terri Oda
http://www.flickr.com/photos/terrio/

Chapter 2 - By: Dekuwa
http://www.flickr.com/photos/dekuwa/

Chapter 3 - By: MIKI Yoshihito
http://www.flickr.com/photos/mujitra/

Chapter 4 - By: Gabri Solera
http://www.flickr.com/photos/besosyflores/

Chapter 5 - By: Cliff
http://www.flickr.com/photos/nostri-imago/

Chapter 6 - By: George Alexander
http://www.flickr.com/photos/garussell11/

Chapter 7 - By: Susi
http://www.flickr.com/photos/sushithegreat/

Chapter 8 - By: Festival Karsh
http://www.flickr.com/photos/festivalkarsh/

Chapter 9 - By: Ronnie Macdonald
http://www.flickr.com/photos/ronmacphotos/

Chapter 10 - By: Brian Beatty
http://www.flickr.com/photos/bcbeatty/

Chapter 11 - By: Sam Howzit
http://www.flickr.com/photos/aloha75/

Chapter 12 - By: Janene at ooobop!
http://www.flickr.com/photos/16375127@N02/

Other Books By The Author

Product Management

- Product Development Lessons For Product Managers: How Product Managers Can Create Successful Products

- Customer Lessons For Product Managers: Techniques For Product Managers To Better Understand What Their Customers Really Want

- Product Failure Lessons For Product Managers: Examples Of Products That Have Failed For Product Managers To Learn From

- Communication Skills For Product Managers: The Communication Skills That Product Managers Need To Know How To Use In Order To Have A Successful Product

- How To Have A Successful Product Manager Career: The Things That You Need To Be Doing TODAY In Order To Have A Successful Product Manager Career

- Product Manager Product Success: How to keep your product on track and make it become a success

Public Speaking

- How To Give A Great Presentation: Presentation techniques that will transform a speech into a memorable event

- How To Rehearse In Order To Give The Perfect Speech: How to effectively rehearse your next speech to that your message be remembered forever!

- Secrets To Creating The Perfect Speech: How to create a speech that will make your message be remembered forever!

- Secrets To Organizing The Perfect Speech: How to organize the best speech of your life!

- Secrets To Planning The Perfect Speech: How to plan to give the best speech of your life

CIO Skills

- How CIOs Can Make Innovation Happen: Tips And Techniques For CIOs To Use In Order To Make Innovation Happen In Their IT Department

- CIO Communication Skills Secrets: Tips And Techniques For CIOs To Use In Order To Become Better Communicators

- Managing Your CIO Career: Steps That CIOs Have To Take In Order To Have A Long And Successful Career

- CIO Business Skills: How CIOs can work effectively with the rest of the company!

IT Manager Skills

- Secrets Of Effective Leadership For IT Managers: Tips And Techniques That IT Managers Can Use In Order To Develop Leadership Skills

- IT Manager Career Secrets: Tips And Techniques That IT Managers Can Use In Order To Have A Successful Career

- IT Manager Budgeting Skills: How IT Managers Can Request, Manage, Use, And Track Their Funding

Negotiating

- Learn How To Argue In Your Next Negotiation: How To Develop The Skill Of Effective Arguing In A Negotiation In Order To Get The Best Possible Outcome

- How To Open Your Next Negotiation: How To Start A Negotiation In Order To Get The Best Possible Outcome

- Preparing For Your Next Negotiation: What You Need To Do BEFORE A Negotiation Starts In Order To Get The Best Possible Deal

Miscellaneous

- Power Distribution Unit (PDU) Secrets: What Everyone Who Works In A Data Center Needs To Know!

- Making The Jump: How To Land Your Dream Job When You Get Out Of College!

Decision Making Skills That Every CIO Needs To Have In Order To Be Able To Make The Right Choices

This book has been written with one goal in mind – to show you how you successfully manage your IT department. It's not easy being a CIO so we're going to show you the strategies and techniques that you can use to make sure that you make the right decisions for your IT department!

Let's Make Your CIO Career A Success!

What You'll Find Inside:

- **IT JUDGMENT CALLS: HOW TO MAKE GOOD ONES**

- **BREAKTHROUGH IT STRATEGY: TAKE A NEW "PATH" TO SUCCESS**

- **W.W.N.M.D.?: WHAT WOULD NELSON MANDELA DO?.**

- **WICKED, WICKED IT STRATEGY PROBLEMS**

Dr. Jim Anderson brings his 25 years of real-world experience to this book. He's been a senior IT executive at some of the world's largest firms. He's going to show you what you need to do (and not do!) in order to make your CIO career a success!

www.ingramcontent.com/pod-product-compliance
Lightning Source LLC
Chambersburg PA
CBHW071810170526
45167CB00003B/1257